Space Technology

Rovers

by Julie Murray

Dash!
LEVELED READERS
An Imprint of Abdo Zoom • abdobooks.com

3

Dash!
LEVELED READERS

Level 1 – Beginning
Short and simple sentences with familiar words or patterns for children who are beginning to understand how letters and sounds go together.

Level 2 – Emerging
Longer words and sentences with more complex language patterns for readers who are practicing common words and letter sounds.

Level 3 – Transitional
More developed language and vocabulary for readers who are becoming more independent.

THIS BOOK CONTAINS RECYCLED MATERIALS

abdobooks.com

Published by Abdo Zoom, a division of ABDO, PO Box 398166, Minneapolis, Minnesota 55439. Copyright © 2020 by Abdo Consulting Group, Inc. International copyrights reserved in all countries. No part of this book may be reproduced in any form without written permission from the publisher. Dash!™ is a trademark and logo of Abdo Zoom.

Printed in the United States of America, North Mankato, Minnesota.
102019
012020

Photo Credits: Alamy, Getty Images, iStock, NASA, Shutterstock, NASA/JPL-Caltech, NASA/JPL-Caltech/MSSS, NASA/JPL/Cornell University
Production Contributors: Kenny Abdo, Jennie Forsberg, Grace Hansen, John Hansen
Design Contributors: Dorothy Toth, Neil Klinepier, Victoria Bates

Library of Congress Control Number: 2019941334

Publisher's Cataloging in Publication Data

Names: Murray, Julie, author.
Title: Rovers / by Julie Murray
Description: Minneapolis, Minnesota : Abdo Zoom, 2020 | Series: Space technology | Includes online resources and index.
Identifiers: ISBN 9781532129278 (lib. bdg.) | ISBN 9781098220259 (ebook) | ISBN 9781098220747 (Read-to-Me ebook)
Subjects: LCSH: Roving vehicles (Astronautics)--Juvenile literature. | Lunar surface vehicles--Juvenile literature. | Space sciences--Juvenile literature. | Technology--Juvenile literature. | Astronautics--Juvenile literature.
Classification: DDC 629.435--dc23

Table of Contents

Rovers

Rovers are vehicles designed to explore the Moon and planets. Some have been driven like a car, while others work like robots.

Rovers can take pictures, collect soil **samples**, and study rocks. They can also record temperature and wind speed.

Moon Missions

The first rover to land on the Moon was Lunokhod 1 in 1970. It was from the **Soviet Union**. It sent more than 20,000 photos back to Earth.

The US sent Lunar Roving Vehicles (LRVs) to the Moon three different times in the early 1970s. The astronauts drove the rovers. The rovers looked like **dune buggies**!

Missions to Mars

Sojourner was the first rover to successfully land on Mars in 1997. It studied soil and rocks on the planet's surface. It sent back hundreds of photos.

Spirit and Opportunity are twin rovers. They landed on Mars in January 2004. They studied opposite sides of the planet. They had cameras, **antennas**, **solar panels**, and robotic arms.

The twin rovers found signs that there may have been water on the planet at one time. Spirit lost contact in March 2010. Opportunity's mission was over in February 2019.

Curiosity landed on Mars in August 2012. It found oxygen, hydrogen, and carbon in rocks on Mars. These are the things needed for life.

19

Mars 2020 is scheduled to launch in the summer of 2020. The rover will carry a drill that can collect core **samples** of rocks and soil. It will look for the potential of life on Mars.

More Facts

- There are more than 70 space crafts on the Moon. They are old rovers, modules, and crashed orbiters.

- Curiosity played the first song on Mars. It played the song "Reach for the Stars" by will.i.am.

- Opportunity was the longest active rover. It was expected to last 90 days. It was "alive" for 15 years!

Glossary

antenna – a metal device that sends or receives signals.

dune buggy – a low, wide-wheeled motor vehicle for recreational driving on many types of terrain.

sample – a small part of something that shows what the whole is like.

solar panel – a panel designed to absorb the sun's rays as a source of energy for generating electricity or heating.

Soviet Union – a country that no longer exists that was made up of fifteen republics in eastern Europe and northern Asia. Moscow was its capital.

Index

Online Resources

Booklinks
NONFICTION NETWORK
FREE! ONLINE NONFICTION RESOURCES

To learn more about rovers, please visit **abdobooklinks.com** or scan this QR code. These links are routinely monitored and updated to provide the most current information available.